What Are the Issues with Genetic Technology?

Eve Hartman and Wendy Meshbesher

Chicago, Illinois

www.capstonepub.com
Visit our website to find out more information about Heinemann-Raintree books.

To order:

☎ Phone 888-454-2279

💻 Visit www.capstonepub.com to browse our catalog and order online.

Edited by Adam Miller, Andrew Farrow, and Adrian Vigliano
Designed by Philippa Jenkins
Original illustrations © Capstone Global Library Limited 2012
Illustrated by Medi-mation p8, KJA-artists.com p30
Picture research by Mica Brancic
Originated by Capstone Global Library Ltd.
Printed and bound in China by CTPS Ltd.

15 14 13 12 11
10 9 8 7 6 5 4 3 2 1

Library of Congress Cataloging-in-Publication Data
Cataloging-in-Publication Data is on file at the Library of Congress.

ISBNs: 978-1-4109-4464-1 (HC) 978-1-4109-4471-9 (PB)

Acknowledgments
The author and publishers are grateful to the following for permission to reproduce copyright material: Alamy p. 35 left (© Lana Sundman); Corbis pp. 5 (epa/© Pedro Armestre), 15 (© John Springer Collection), 22 (epa/© Jon Hrusa), 29 (© Owen Franken), 31 (© Reuters/ Jeff J Mitchell), 43 (© Tim Pannell); Getty Images pp. 10 (Taxi/Shioguchi), 11 (Bloomberg/Jack Plunkett), 12 (Bloomberg/Daniel Acker), 24 (Flickr/Christian Senger), 39 (The Image Bank/Tim Kitchen), 20 left (Close-up of a baby boy); Reuters p. 41 (Heinz-Peter Bader); Science Photo Library pp. 9 (Edward Kinsman), 13 (US Department Of Energy/Oak Ridge National Laboratory), 14 (Eye of Science), 38 (Visuals Unlimited/ Margaret Oechsli), 20 right (AJ Photo), 6 bottom (Eye of Science); Shutterstock pp. 4 (© Vivid Pixels), 7 (© Pavel Shchegolev), 17 (© Alexander Raths), 18 (© Mikhail Tchkheidze), 19 (© Marcel Jancovic), 25 (© Dirtfoto), 26 (© Veniamin Kraskov), 27 (© Henk Bentlage), 32 (© Shawn Hempel), 34 (© Jonathan Feinstein), 37 (© Krasowit), 35 right (© imagelab), 6 top (© Pixshots), Contents page bottom (© Shawn Hempel), Contents page top (© Veniamin Kraskov). All background design feature pictures courtesy of Shutterstock.

Main cover photograph of cloning research reproduced with permission of Science Photo Library (Mauro Fermariello); inset cover photograph of a chromosome reproduced with permission of Shutterstock (© Sashkin).

The publisher would like to thank literary consultant Nancy Harris and content consultant Ann Fullick for their assistance in the preparation of this book.

Every effort has been made to contact copyright holders of material reproduced in this book. Any omissions will be rectified in subsequent printings if notice is given to the publisher.

Contents

Why do blue roses cause such controversy?

Find out on page 14!

How can DNA send you to prison, or get you out of prison?

Turn to page 32 to find out!

Some words are shown in bold, **like this**. These words are explained in the glossary. You will find important information and definitions underlined, <u>like this</u>.

GENETIC TECHNOLOGY

Genetic technology could offer choices to parents about their babies.

If you were a parent, would you want to choose features for your baby? Would you choose the color of the baby's eyes or hair, or choose the gender? Maybe you want the baby to have a budding talent in math, music, or sports. Scientists are studying how to choose or change the features of plants and animals, including humans. Some of these choices are already possible to make, even for human babies. More choices may be possible soon. But should they be? Scientists and the public have only just begun to discuss this question.

GENES AND SCIENCE

Genes are the units that pass from parents to offspring and that determine **traits**. A trait is a clear feature of an **organism** (living thing). Physical traits include height, skin color, and possessing a feature such as dimples. Other traits include behavior patterns such as the mating behavior of animals or the time of year a flower blooms.

Scientists have been studying genes and traits for over 100 years. However, within the past 20 years, scientists have discovered ways to change and alter genes. They can also transfer them from one organism to another. **Genetic technology**, which is also called genetic engineering, involves changing or using genes in ways that do not occur in nature.

Today, many farm crops have been **genetically modified** to increase their resistance to pests. Genes of **bacteria** (tiny living things) have been modified to produce useful products, such as **insulin**. Insulin is a substance that the body makes to help control blood sugar levels.

CONTROVERSY!

Not everyone agrees that genetic technology is worthwhile. Many opponents are concerned that the technology could produce dangerous or unwanted organisms. Others argue that it brings more damage than benefit, especially to food crops. Many people object to the technology on moral and ethical grounds (issues of right versus wrong).

You will learn more about these controversies as you continue reading this book.

Genetically modifed food crops are especially controversial.

WHAT ARE GENES?

Genes explain the similarities among these Siberian husky puppies. They explain the differences, too.

The idea of **genes** was proposed in the 1860s by Gregor Mendel, an Austrian monk. Many years later, improvements to microscopes allowed scientists to identify and locate genes in the **cell**. A cell is the smallest building block of a living thing. Genes are found on **chromosomes**. A chromosome is made of a **molecule** called deoxyribonucleic acid or **DNA**. Each gene is a small section of DNA. Almost every cell contains two sets of chromosomes, one from each parent.

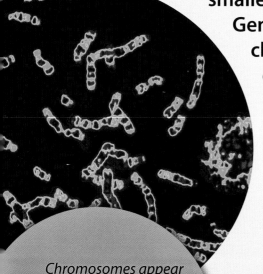

Chromosomes appear as worm-like strands when stained and magnified.

The chromosomes are found in the **nucleus** of the cell. When a cell divides it forms two identical cells. When the cell is getting ready to divide, each chromosome acts as a model for the formation of a new, identical chromosome. Each new cell then gets an identical set of chromosomes containing the same genes.

A human cell has 46 chromosomes. Each chromosome contains between a few hundred and many thousands of genes. They hold a total of between 20,000 and 25,000 genes.

GENES ARE EVERYWHERE!

Scientists have studied the cells of all sorts of **organisms**, from single-celled **bacteria** to whales and elephants. In all of these organisms, genes are organized on chromosomes in much the same way as in the human cell.

In bacteria, the chromosome is circular. It is not stored in a nucleus. But as in all organisms, the chromosome contains the set of genes that the bacterial cell needs to survive.

Genes can affect height, but strength and skills develop only with training.

Chromosome number

Every species has a characteristic number of chromosomes in its cells. Do large, advanced species have more chromosomes per cell than simple species? The chart suggests the answer.

Species	Chromosomes per cell
Corn (Zea mays)	20
Green algae (A.mediterranea)	20
Human (Homo sapiens)	46
Dog (Canis familiaris)	78
Goldfish (Carassius auratus)	94

DNA

DNA is the molecule that makes up genes. Compared to other molecules, a molecule of DNA is huge. Yet how can a molecule of any size control the **traits** of the body? The answer lies in the way the parts of DNA are put together.

DNA contains four different parts called **bases** which pair up neatly. The order of these bases acts as a code for making changes in your body. Different genes result in different traits such as eye color, height, and the age at which you are likely to have your teenage growth spurt.

DNA also plays a role in cancer and other diseases. Certain genes increase the risk of developing cancer of the breast or ovaries. Scientists are finding more and more diseases that are affected by our genes.

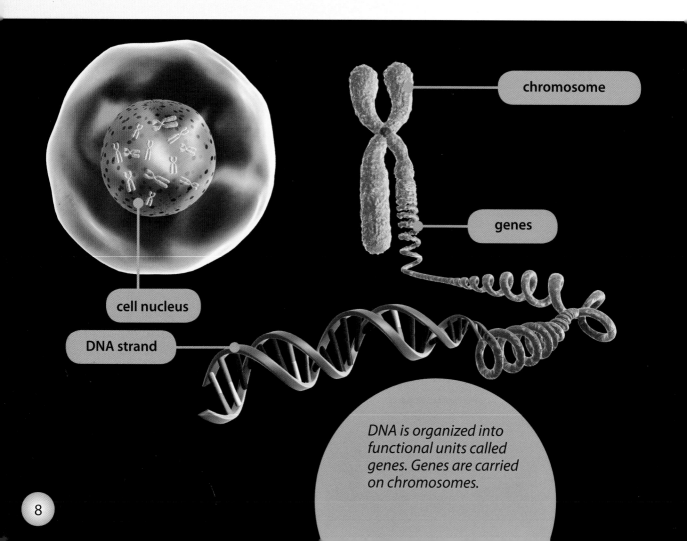

chromosome

genes

cell nucleus

DNA strand

DNA is organized into functional units called genes. Genes are carried on chromosomes.

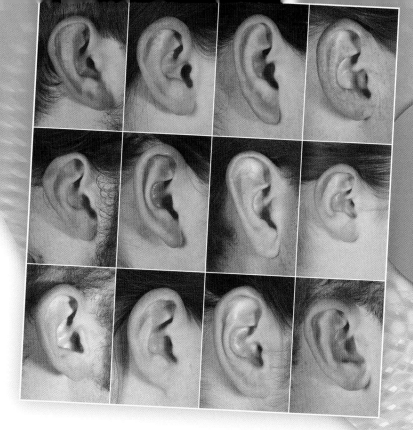

From person to person, subtle differences in DNA affect ear shape and other facial traits.

HUMAN VS. MOUSE

You could easily tell a human and a mouse apart. Humans don't look like trees or dandelions, either. So you might think that these organisms have very different DNA. If so, you would be wrong!

The genetic code is the same for nearly all organisms, as is the process for translating it. As for the DNA itself, many regions of it are identical in plant and animal cells. A human and a mouse have 99 percent of their DNA in common.

The fact that the DNA of most organisms is very similar makes many kinds of **genetic technology** possible. This is because a gene which works in one organism can often be made to work in another organism. This is the basis of genetic engineering.

Junk DNA

As scientists studied DNA, they were surprised to observe that genes take up only a small fraction of the molecule. Most DNA does not appear to do very much. This part of DNA is called junk DNA. Is junk DNA necessary or important? Scientists continue to ponder and investigate this question.

WHAT GENES CONTROL

Just what traits of the human body do genes control? Genes clearly control eye color, hair color, and the shape and size of toes and fingers. Genes also affect height. However, a poor diet or poor general health can affect the height that the body grows to.

Evidence also shows that genes affect personality and intelligence. Talents in math, music, or art have been observed to run in families, even among children who were separated from their biological parents.

IDENTICAL STRANGERS

Identical twins have exactly the same DNA. By studying twins, scientists can study the extent that genes affect or influence human life.

As infants, identical twins Paula Bernstein and Elyse Schein were adopted by different families. They met for the first time at age 35. They discovered they had similar tastes in music and books, and similar personalities. Yet they also realized they had different values based on their different experiences.

Together the twins wrote *Identical Strangers*, a book about their separation and reunion.

By studying identical twins, scientists hope to learn how genes affect thinking and behavior.

The Human Genome Project

Between 1990 and 2003, scientists around the world worked to identify every code in human DNA. Scientists are still analyzing the data. They are already using some of the information in practical ways to help them understand and treat genetic diseases. One day they hope to be able to cure them.

One benefit of the Human Genome Project is new technology for sequencing genes. By 2020, a machine might be able to sequence the DNA of an individual human in about 15 minutes! Doctors could use the information to treat patients.

The brown calf is a clone, or genetic duplicate, of its parent (not pictured). You will read more about cloning on page 30.

GENETIC TECHNOLOGY TODAY

Some technologies develop slowly and gradually. This is not the case with **genetic technology**! In the past 20 years, scientists have developed and applied genetic technology that affects people everywhere. Foods, drugs, and medical treatments all come from this technology. As you will discover, though, the technology raises issues about science and **ethics** (the study of right and wrong).

The genes of these corn plants have been altered to help them resist pests.

TRANSGENIC ORGANISMS

In many processes of genetic technology, a useful **gene** is transferred from one **organism** to another. The organisms are often from very different species. Genes from **bacteria** have been transferred to plants and to animals.

Organisms made from transferred genes are called **transgenic organisms**. A transgenic corn plant or sugar beet may look or behave very much like any other plant of its species. But the transferred gene provides a new **trait**, such as resistance to pests.

KNOCKOUTS

Scientists are also using genetic technology to learn how genes operate. One simple way of testing a gene's function is to remove it from the organism. Scientists call the new organism a **knockout**.

As you've already read, mice and humans share about 99 percent of the same genes. To learn how human genes work, scientists have been studying knockout mice. By comparing the knockout mouse to normal mice, scientists can figure out the gene's function in both mice and humans.

Altering a single gene can cause drastic changes, such as a tripling of body size.

This mouse glows in the dark because of a gene it received from a glowing jellyfish.

Blue roses

By using **conventional methods**, plant scientists and gardeners have bred roses that are red, white, yellow, and shades in between. But a blue color does not occur naturally in roses, so breeding a blue rose was not possible—until genetic technology arrived.

Scientists have now created blue roses (see the photo on page 26). They also have made other unusual living things, such as a fish that glows in the dark. Some people argue that these products are an improper use of genetic technology. Many people argue against these products on ethical or moral grounds. What do you think?

GENETICALLY MODIFIED CROPS

Today, much of the world's corn and sugar crops are grown from **genetically modified (GM)** plants. These plants were given genes that make them resistant to pests or drought. They are examples of **transgenic plants**, or plants that include genes from other organisms.

One common gene that is now in food crops comes from a type of bacteria. In bacteria, the gene produces a substance that kills young insects that feed on it. The gene now does the same thing in transgenic corn and potatoes, and other crops.

In another chapter you will read much more about GM crops and the controversy surrounding them.

SPIDERS AND MONSTERS?

In a popular movie, the hero is bitten by a GM spider. Soon he can spin webs and climb walls like a spider can. However, this is possible only in fiction. Genetic technology is not likely to create monsters because the genes for such creatures do not exist.

Some seemingly simple **traits**, such as eye color in humans, depend on many genes that work together in complicated ways. So although an isolated gene can be transferred to a new organism, a large set of genes for a complex trait, such as a head or limb, cannot.

Humans turning into insects or other creatures is a popular theme in science fiction. But it cannot happen in real life, even with genetic technology.

PHARMING

Pharmaceuticals are drugs and medicines. In a practice called **pharming**, scientists use transgenic plants or animals to produce a pharmaceutical. Often the "pharmed" drug is a chemical made normally by the human body.

In one pharming technique, a human gene is transferred to a cow, goat, or other **mammal**. The animal then makes the product of this gene and releases it in its milk. Scientists then collect the product from the milk.

Drugs are made by transgenic bacteria and plants, too. **Insulin** is an example. Insulin is the chemical that helps the body process blood sugar. Human insulin from transgenic organisms can be used to treat **diabetes**. Diabetes is a disease in which the body does not produce enough insulin of its own. When diabetes is not controlled, every organ (body part such as the heart or liver) in the body can be harmed.

Better insulin

Diabetes affects 200 million people worldwide, and the number is growing every year. In the past, insulin for diabetics was expensive and not always of high quality. Pharming can provide effective, low-cost insulin that is chemically identical to human insulin.

RIGHT OR WRONG?

Genetic technology is new, and so are the ethical questions it raises. Is it right to change the genes of plants and animals, even for noble purposes such as improving human health? People are forming different answers to this question. As you read on, try to consider both sides of ethical issues as you form your own opinions about them.

People with diabetes depend on injections of insulin. Genetic technology could provide insulin of high quality and low cost.

FROM PARENTS TO CHILDREN

Scientists have amassed a huge body of knowledge about human **genes**, both from **genetic technology** and other sources. Scientists can now evaluate the genes of babies before they are born. As genetic technology advances, **genetic disorders** (illnesses caused by genes) might disappear from the human population. Other genetic changes are also possible.

A baby's genes can be assessed well before birth. But are genetic assessments worthwhile?

GENETIC COUNSELING AND TESTS

As we've discussed, genes interact with each other in complicated ways. It is possible that two healthy parents could have a child that suffers from a genetic disorder. The gene for this disorder could be hidden in both parents, then become a problem in the child.

In **genetic counseling**, a geneticist or other expert analyzes the possibility of genetic disorders in a couple's future children. Many couples use genetic counseling to help them decide whether to have children.

A pregnant woman may decide to test the genes of the fetus (developing baby) she is carrying. These tests also help detect genetic disorders that affect whole **chromosomes**, such as Down syndrome. They also help detect genetic disorders that are linked to the sex of the baby.

Too much information?

People can have their genes tested for many diseases, including Huntington's disease (a loss of nerve function) and Alzheimer's disease (a brain disorder that involves memory loss). Other tests can assess a person's risk of developing certain forms of cancer.

These tests offer both benefits and drawbacks. The results can help patients plan their lives and make important decisions, such as whether to have children. Yet the results can raise fears and anxiety. And what if a patient loses medical insurance because of test results?

Science alone cannot decide whether genetic testing is the right choice. Individuals must choose for themselves.

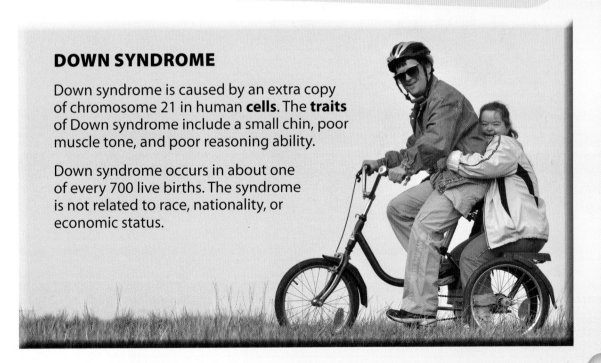

DOWN SYNDROME

Down syndrome is caused by an extra copy of chromosome 21 in human **cells**. The **traits** of Down syndrome include a small chin, poor muscle tone, and poor reasoning ability.

Down syndrome occurs in about one of every 700 live births. The syndrome is not related to race, nationality, or economic status.

DESIGNER BABIES?

All over the world, scientists are changing the genes of **bacteria**, plants, and animals such as cows, goats, and mice. But for the most part, changing human genes is illegal. Laws of many nations prevent the creation of a transgenic human baby. Nevertheless, many actions that affect a baby's genetics are legal and common. They are carried out to try and prevent the birth of children affected by serious genetic diseases which will shorten their lives.

Fertility is the ability to conceive or bear children. Many fertility clinics help parents conceive a baby through artifical means. In a process called **in vitro fertilization (IVF)**, sperm and egg cells are united outside the body. The tiny embryos that start to grow can be genetically tested before they are put back inside their mother, to make sure they are healthy. People who want to donate (give) eggs or sperm to infertile people can be genetically tested to make sure they do not carry genetic diseases.

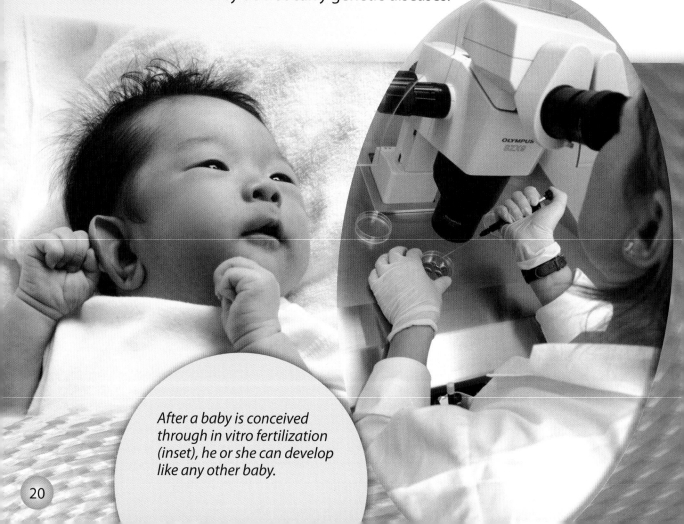

After a baby is conceived through in vitro fertilization (inset), he or she can develop like any other baby.

MORE QUESTIONS

When you read the term "designer baby," what comes to mind? Maybe you think of a baby who is designed like a living room, with any desired combination of traits. But this type of design is not possible, and wouldn't be even if it were legal. Many genetic techniques that are legal for mice and other animals are illegal for humans. And everything that is allowed is designed to result in a healthy baby.

Nevertheless, scientists and others are concerned about the real issues that genetic technology raises for the human race. The methods used to select healthy embryos could be used to choose the sex of a baby because the parents wanted a boy or a girl, not to avoid genetic diseases. Is this a good idea? Should parents be allowed to choose the color of their baby's eyes even if it is possible? What if scientists could effectively test sperm and eggs for traits such as intelligence or musical ability? Should such tests even be performed? Questions like these could become important in your lifetime.

"I think it's very important that we do not bury our head in the sand and pretend these advances are not happening."

—Dr. Jeffrey Steinberg, director of a fertility institute

GENETICALLY MODIFIED CROPS

Farmers are now growing a variety of **genetically modified (GM)** crops, especially in the United States. In Europe, however, opposition to GM crops is greater, and they are less common there. Companies that develop GM crops insist that their products are effectively identical to unmodified crops. Yet critics strongly disagree. The controversy continues, and the outcome will affect the world food supply for many years.

Many nations face shortages of food. Experts disagree about whether GM crops can help solve this problem.

ARGUMENTS FOR...

As you have read, genetic modification can help crop plants resist pests and drought (severe lack of rain). They also can be made to resist **herbicides**, which are chemicals that kill weeds.

In theory, these qualities make GM crops easier and more economical to grow. On a large farm, huge sums of money are invested to plant seeds and raise crops. In theory, GM crops help farmers receive a better return for their investment and labor, and ensure that the world receives food from the farm.

GM crops can also be made to be more nutritious. A GM strain of rice has been made to produce vitamin A. The future may bring other vitamin-enhanced crops.

...AND AGAINST

Critics argue that GM crops are not necessary, and that they are dangerous to both the environment and human health.

The techniques of **genetic technology** have been compared to performing heart surgery with a garden shovel. A transferred **gene** could affect an **organism** in unintended ways. The damage might take many generations to appear.

Critics cite studies that show that GM peas caused an allergic reaction in mice, evidence that genetic modification can change foods for the worse. Other studies suggest that GM foods are less nutritious than unmodified foods. Critics are also concerned that GM crops will breed with other crops, permanently changing them in unknown ways.

SAFETY CONCERNS

Look again at the photo shown on page 15. Genetic monsters like this one are not a real concern. Scientists also doubt that **genetic technology** could create a human monster, even if such technology were legal on humans. However, scientists have many real concerns about safety, especially from **GM** crops.

Bees spread pollen from flower to flower. They could spread genes from GM crops to wild plants.

Farms are not isolated from nature. GM plants can easily spread from the fields where they are grown.

GENETIC POLLUTION

Transgenic organisms could cause problems if their **genes** "escaped" into new **organisms**. This kind of gene spread is called **genetic pollution**.

When a GM crop is grown, it does not merely provide food for humans. Honeybees feed on the crop, as do birds and other wild animals. The genes could transfer to these animals, with unknown consequences.

GM crops also spread their new genes in **pollen**. Pollen has to go from one flower to another for plants to reproduce. Through insects, birds, and the wind, pollen can travel from crop plants to wild plants. New genes could easily enter the environment in this way. Again, no one is certain what the effect would be.

Unlike other kinds of pollution, genetic pollution may be impossible to clean up. Once a gene escapes into the wild, it might be there permanently.

Slow down?

The first GM crop, a variety of tomato, was introduced in 1994. Within a few years, many more crops were developed and raised. Many critics argue that long-term testing should have been conducted to determine the safety and value of these crops. They still want these tests conducted today.

25

ETHICAL ISSUES

Ethics is the study of right versus wrong. You already have read about many of these questions, and there are many more. As with other questions of ethics, the ethical questions raised by **genetic technology** are often difficult to answer. Sometimes an answer to one question leads to more questions that are even harder to answer.

IS IT RIGHT?

Is it right for humans to change the **genes** of plants and animals? Before you decide the answer, consider the fact that humans have always made such changes. This is how most of our familiar farm crops and animals came into existence.

In a process called **selective breeding**, a human breeder chooses parent plants or animals to mate. The parents have desirable **traits**, and these traits are passed to offspring. In this way, strains of corn have been bred for sweet, tasty kernels. Cattle have been bred for either their milk or meat.

People created blue roses using genetic technology. Some people have questioned the ethics of this.

Breeding has also created new kinds of animals. Donkeys and horses are mated to produce mules. People have also mated horses with zebras.

Dairy cattle are the result of many years of selective breeding.

THE ETHICAL DIFFERENCE

If selective breeding is acceptable, what might make genetic technology unacceptable? Does the fact that genetic technology involves scientists and laboratories make a difference? If a gene from **bacteria** could naturally transfer to a plant or animal, would that make it acceptable for scientists to perform the same transfer in laboratories?

As you consider these questions, remember that selective breeding still relies on chance. It also changes species in very limited ways. The genes of a fish and a plant would never mingle together in nature, but it could happen with genetic technology.

"[Genetic engineering] is a matter far too important to be left solely in the hands of the scientific and medical communities."

—James D. Watson, *codiscoverer of the structure of DNA*

27

HUMAN HEALTH

Genetic technology is now being used to create new medicines and therapies for many disorders and diseases. In the future, the impact of genetic technology may even be greater.

GENE THERAPY

A **genetic disorder** is a condition in which **genes** cause the body to function poorly. Some genetic disorders, such as Down syndrome, arise when **chromosomes** form or develop abnormally. Other disorders are inherited, or come to a child from a parent's genes.

Cystic fibrosis is an inherited disorder that is caused by a single defective gene. This defective gene causes the body to produce very thick, sticky mucus. The mucus clogs the lungs and breathing passages.

To treat cystic fibrosis, scientists are now experimenting with **gene therapy**. Gene therapy is any technique that uses genes to treat a disease or disorder. Scientists are experimenting with ways to deliver the normal gene to a patient's lungs. The treatment is promising because it treats the cause of cystic fibrosis, not the symptoms.

THE RISKS OF GENE THERAPY

Like other experimental treatments on humans, gene therapy offers both rewards and risks. One risk comes from the **vector**, or carrier, of the gene that the patient receives. Viruses (tiny disease-causing **organisms**) might make ideal vectors, but they also can cause serious infections.

In 1999, 18-year-old Jesse Gelsinger became the first person to die in a test for gene therapy. Jesse suffered from a rare genetic disorder that affected the liver. He died because of his body's response to the virus used in the therapy.

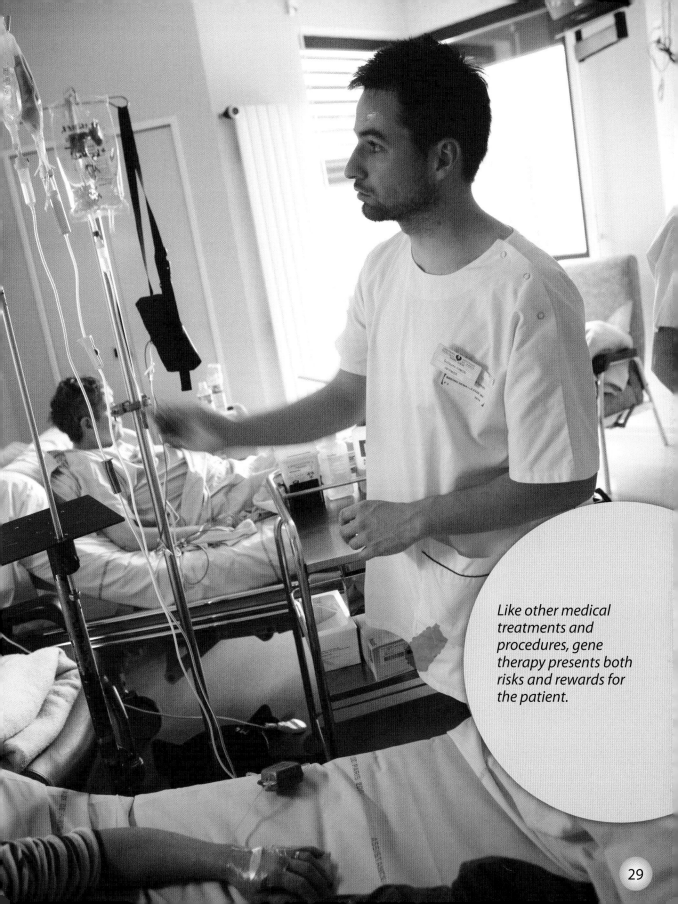

Like other medical treatments and procedures, gene therapy presents both risks and rewards for the patient.

CLONING

A **clone** is an exact genetic duplicate. Scientists have successfully cloned many animals, but also have had many failures. As cloning technology improves, cloned farm animals, pets, and wild animals may become very common. Not surprisingly, many people have strong opinions about whether cloning should be allowed—especially on humans.

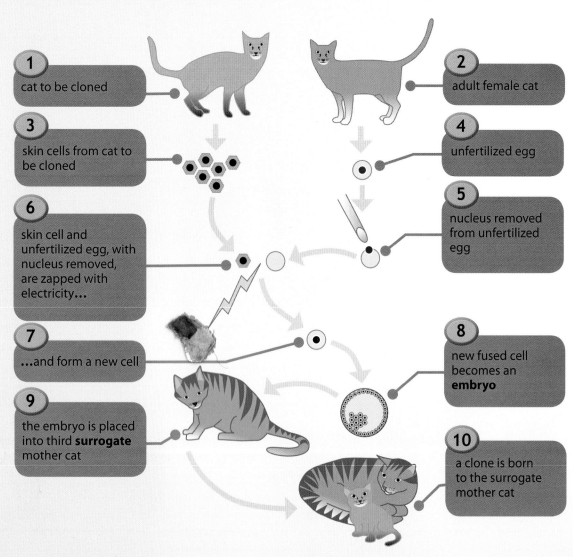

1 cat to be cloned

2 adult female cat

3 skin cells from cat to be cloned

4 unfertilized egg

5 nucleus removed from unfertilized egg

6 skin cell and unfertilized egg, with nucleus removed, are zapped with electricity...

7 ...and form a new cell

8 new fused cell becomes an **embryo**

9 the embryo is placed into third **surrogate** mother cat

10 a clone is born to the surrogate mother cat

DOLLY THE SHEEP

In 1996, after over 200 failed attempts, scientists succeeded in creating Dolly, a cloned sheep. Dolly was not the first cloned animal. But she was the first clone of an adult **mammal**. Her successful birth raised the possibility of cloning any adult animal for any purpose.

Dolly died in 2003. She lived a normal life that included giving birth to lambs. Although scientists have cloned other farm animals, cloning remains experimental and not practical.

HUMAN CLONING

With new technology, scientists can clone human **cells**. Now they hope to use cloned human cells to repair damaged body parts such as an injured spinal cord. In theory, cloned cells could also remake a whole body. A fertilized human egg that is cloned could grow and develop inside the mother's body, the same way any other human baby develops.

The cloning of humans is illegal in many nations. Many ethicists and religious leaders have criticized the entire concept. Do you agree? What is your opinion?

IT'S NOT SO EASY

At first glance, the technique for cloning seems simple. First, scientists take an egg from an animal and remove the genetic contents. **Genes** from the donor are then inserted, replacing the original genes, and a clone is made.

Yet for reasons scientists do not quite understand, this technique fails much more often than it succeeds. Dogs have proved especially hard to clone. Chickens and monkeys have proved even more difficult. Animals often die during the experiments.

Dolly, the first cloned sheep, lived and looked like any other sheep.

DNA FINGERPRINTING

As you now know, most **DNA** is the same from animal to animal. Among humans, nearly all DNA is the same. However, scientists have identified specific regions of DNA that differ from person to person. These differences are analyzed in a technique called **DNA fingerprinting**, which is used to identify people. DNA fingerprinting is used as evidence in court cases and to identify family relationships. The technology also raises many ethical and legal questions.

This researcher is examining information taken from DNA. Procedures like this can be used to find evidence that can be used in court.

EVIDENCE FROM DNA

Soon after a baby is born, hospital staff press the baby's hands or feet in ink and then make a print. Everyone has a unique set of whirls and ridges on his or her fingers and toes. The pattern can be used to identify each person.

DNA fingerprinting works in much the same way. Scientists can obtain DNA from blood or any tissue sample, such as skin. By comparing the DNA from two samples, they can determine whether or not the samples came from the same donor.

Evidence from DNA has led to guilty and not-guilty verdicts in many cases. Some people who have been in prison for 20 years or longer have had their innocence proven by DNA evidence.

Private property?

In the United States, the military stores DNA samples of all soldiers and issues DNA-based identification tags. Security experts have suggested that DNA be used to identify civilians (people who aren't in the military), too.

Does your DNA belong to you? Is it completely private property, or does society have a right to register it? These questions may become very important in the years ahead.

GENES AND THE LAW

Are enough laws in place to regulate **genetic technology**? Do existing laws reflect the advances and discoveries of the technology? Many experts say the answer to both questions is no. Genetic technology is developing rapidly, perhaps faster than the laws that apply to it. Today, new discoveries are forcing judges to question the laws and rulings that made sense 20 or 30 years ago.

In the United States, GM foods are sold with no special labels or identification. Do you think the laws should be changed?

"Sugar, High Fructose Corn Syrup, Water, Enri
Flour (Wheat Flour, Niacin, Reduced Iron, T'
[Vitamin B1] Riboflavin [Vitamin B2] Folic
Hydrogenated Soybean and Cottonseed O
Preserve Flavor (Contributes a Trivial Amou
Palm and Palm Kernel Oil, Dextrose, cocoa, Eg
Oil, Colors (Caramel Color, Red 40) Emulsifiers (Sorbita
Monostearate, Polysorbate 60, Mono- and Diglycerides
Soy Lecithin) Whey (Milk) Leavening (Baking Soda, Sod
Aluminum Phosphate) Salt, Corn Starch, Sorbic Acid (to
Retain Freshness) Natural and Artificial Flavors, Egg Wh

GENETICALLY MODIFIED PRODUCT

Many consumers accept or reject a food based on its ingredients and preparation, including genetic modification.

A CHANGE TO PATENT LAWS

A **patent** is a legal document that gives an inventor the exclusive rights to an invention. Patents are important. Companies or individuals can invest time and money into their inventions because they know a patent will be available.

For many years, governments would not give patents for things found in nature. Then, in 1980, the U.S. Supreme Court ruled in favor of Ananda Chakrabarty, a scientist who had developed an **organism** for cleaning oil spills. This was the first time any government had granted a patent for a living organism. Since then, courts all over the world have granted thousands of patents for **genes** and **transgenic organisms**.

In the 1980 decision, one of the key science arguments was that genes had very predictable effects, and these effects stayed the same from organism to organism. Scientists now know that this idea is incorrect. The same gene may operate in different ways in a bacterium, a plant, and an animal. Nevertheless, patents for individual genes continue to be granted.

Seeds in court

Monsanto is an international company that makes and sells **GM** seeds. The company has accused many farmers of stealing these seeds. The farmers insist that the seeds drifted into their fields from neighboring farms. They are accusing Monsanto of genetic pollution!

In California, a new law is helping to protect the farmers' rights. But the controversy continues.

GENES AND THE FUTURE

Scientists continue to make discoveries and breakthroughs in **genetic technology**. As genetic technology advances and becomes more widespread, its impact on society will continue to increase. Here are four examples of issues that could become very important in the future. Some are already important today!

GM FOOD ANIMALS

Many animals have been **genetically modified (GM)**. Most are either kept in laboratories, such as **knockout** mice, or used for **pharming**, such as the sheep which make blood clotting proteins in their milk. Now scientists have created GM salmon. If approved, the salmon would be the first GM animal to be used for food.

The AquAdvantage® Salmon has **genes** that allow it to grow faster and larger than other salmon. The company that owns the **patent** claims that the salmon's eggs are infertile, meaning they will not hatch. But some scientists dispute this claim.

Questions

Is GM salmon safe to eat? Could its altered genes escape into fish populations in the wild? If so, how would those populations change?

GENETIC TESTING AND DISCRIMINATION

Can a company refuse to hire an employee because of a genetic test? Can an insurance company refuse to help someone or charge more because of such tests? In the United States and Europe, the answer to both questions is no. In most cases, laws now protect the privacy of genetic tests. But discrimination still occurs.

For example, the U.S. military can deny health benefits to soldiers who suffer from certain genetic diseases. For this reason, some military doctors are advising soldiers to avoid genetic testing of any kind.

Questions

Would you want your employer to know the results of a genetic test? Do you think discrimination occurs because of a person's genes, despite the laws against it?

GM salmon could be the first genetically-modified animal approved as food.

EPIGENETICS

Humans have around 20,000 to 25,000 genes. But different sets of genes are active in every **cell**, and different genes are active at different times. **Epigenetics** is the study of how factors in the environment can affect genes. These factors include diet and stress.

By studying epigenetics, scientists hope to develop drugs that could "turn off" the genes that play a role in diseases. The drugs could help treat diseases such as cancer, autism, and Alzheimer's.

The study of epigenetics has already provided evidence for a new idea about genetic inheritance. As scientists know very well, people can shorten their lives with behaviors such as heavy smoking or overeating. Yet these actions also affect the genes, and the genetic damage can pass from parent to child.

Questions

Should scientists pursue genetic treatments for diseases?

Azacitidine, shown here in crystalized form, is the first epigenetic drug.

STEM CELL RESEARCH

More than 100 trillion cells make up the adult human body. These cells are highly specialized, meaning they have different structures that let them do different jobs. Cells in muscle tissue, for example, look different and function differently than cells in bones and the blood.

In contrast, cells that appear very early in development are not differentiated. These are **stem cells**, the cells that grow into the wide variety and huge number of cells in the body.

Scientists around the world are now studying stem cells and how their genes function. The hope is that stem cells could help humans regrow injured or lost cells, such as from brain or spinal cord injuries. But stem cell research is controversial. Useful stem cells come from early stages of human life. Not everyone agrees that stem cell research is ethical.

Questions

What do you think about the ethics of stem cell research?

If damaged nerves could be regenerated, this basketball player could walk again.

CHANGING THE RULES

For many years, scientists thought that the chemicals of living things behaved very differently from other chemicals. Then, in 1828, German chemist Friedrich Wohler synthesized (made) **urea** in his laboratory. Urea is the waste product that the liver makes. Scientists of the time thought that Wohler's accomplishment was impossible!

Today, **genetic technology** has led to many events that were once thought impossible. Corn plants are making their own pesticides. **Bacteria** are making human **insulin**. Parents can choose the gender of their child to avoid terrible genetic diseases. Many rules about life that once seemed valid no longer apply.

...TO WHAT END?

So what comes next? What old rules about life will scientists discover can be broken? And what benefits or drawbacks will these discoveries bring? Only time will tell.

Whether or not you become a scientist, your opinion matters about the direction of science and technology. Scientists will continue to study and investigate how **organisms** live, grow, and function. Whether this knowledge should be developed into new technology, and how such technology should be used, are issues for everyone in society to decide.

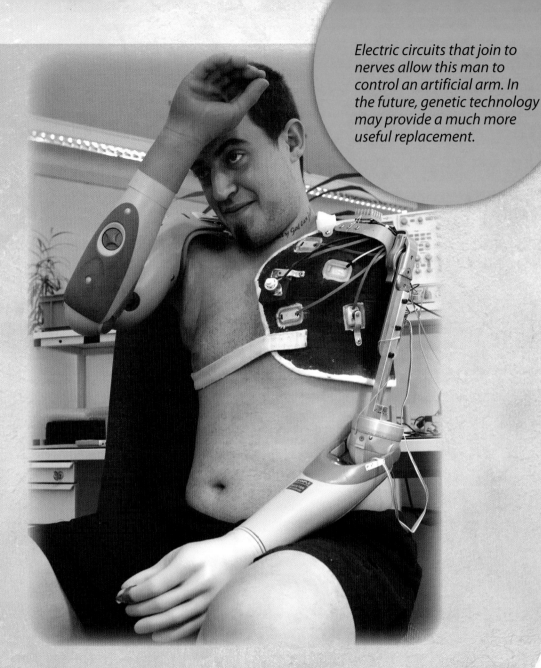

Electric circuits that join to nerves allow this man to control an artificial arm. In the future, genetic technology may provide a much more useful replacement.

ARTIFICIAL LIMBS

Years ago, an artificial arm or leg was merely a stick of wood or plastic. Today, such limbs are highly technical devices. In many cases, the person can use his or her nervous system to control the motion of the limb. Nevertheless, even the most advanced artificial limb is less useful than the original.

Could the body be made to regrow a lost limb? Or could **nerves** be regrown and trained to operate an artificial limb? Genetic technology could make this possible.

SUMMARY

Genetic technology is a rapidly developing branch of science. Major advances have been made within the past 20 years. Many more advances are likely in the near future.

Scientists have now created dozens of **transgenic organisms**, meaning they have transferred **genes** from one organism to another. Transgenic farm crops have been made with genes from other plants and **bacteria** that provide resistance to pests and drought. Transgenic microorganisms, plants, and animals have been made with genes from the human body for useful products, such as **insulin**.

Although altering human genes is illegal, genetic technology is used to analyze human genes and predict genetic **traits**. Experiments on mice show how human genes function. The results could lead to new treatments for diseases and for **genetic disorders**.

Yet genetic technology is not without risks and drawbacks. Many people argue that GM food crops are harmful to the environment and human health. Many people also object to all types of genetic technology for ethical reasons.

RESEARCH TOPICS

Look online or in printed reference sources for information on these topics. If you want to find out more about genetic technology, try researching some of these topics.

DNA, here shown in a model, is the basis of all genetic technology.

NEW TRANSGENIC ORGANISMS
GM plants and animals are being developed every day. Some are intended for laboratory research, others for the supermarket. Search for transgenic bacteria, transgenic sheep, transgenic mice or transgenic plants.

NEW GENE THERAPIES Scientists continue studying **gene therapies** for treating **genetic disorders**. Research their progress in cystic fibrosis or SCID gene therapy.

NEW LAWS AND COURT CASES All over the world, governments are debating laws that affect **genetic technology** and its use. Search for laws, judges, and genetic technology.

NEW DISCOVERIES Scientists continue studying the **DNA** and **genes** of humans and other **organisms**. Their discoveries can overturn old ideas. Search for genetic technology discoveries.

NEW CONCERNS Scientists, government leaders, and citizens groups continue to evaluate genetic technology and its consequences. Search for genetic technology **ethics**.

Glossary

bacteria single-celled microorganism

base basic unit that makes up DNA

cell smallest parts, or building blocks, of a plant or animal

chromosome structure that contains genes; carried in the cell nucleus

clone exact genetic duplicate of an organism

diabetes disease in which the body does not make or process insulin appropriately

DNA deoxyribonucleic acid, the molecule that codes for traits in all organisms

DNA fingerprinting technique in which DNA is analyzed to identify an individual

embryo tiny bundle of cells, that is formed in the first few days of a new human's or animal's development

epigenetics study of how the environment affects genes and gene expression

ethics study of right and wrong

fertilization process of an egg cell joining with a sperm cell, creating the potential for an embryo to develop in the right conditions

fertility ability to have children or offspring

gene part of the genetic information of a living thing. Most genes tell cells how to make a particular protein.

gene therapy use of genetic technology to treat a disease or illness

genetic counseling providing information about genes and helping people make decisions that relate to genes

genetic disorder illness or condition caused by atypical genes

genetic pollution spread of harmful or unwanted genes into the wild

genetic technology change or study of an organism's genes for a useful purpose

genetically modified (GM) genes that have been artificially altered

herbicide chemical that kills weeds or other small plants

in vitro fertilization (IVF) joining of egg and sperm in an artificial environment, such as a test tube

insulin chemical the body makes to help control blood sugar levels

knockout organism from which one gene was removed

mammal warm-blooded animal that makes milk for its young

molecule group of atoms bonded together

nerve body tissue that transmits electrical signals

nucleus membrane-bound structure in the cell that contains chromosomes

organism individual living thing

patent legal document that provides the rights to an invention

pharming using genetically-modified organisms to produce drugs or medicines

pollen powder that plants make to reproduce

selective breeding choosing parents with desired traits to mate

stem cell cell that can divide to produce very specific cells, such as nerve cells

surrogate female who carries a developing fetus, which has been created using an egg cell from a different female

trait characteristic or feature of an organism

transgenic organism organism made from transferred genes

transgenic plant plant to which one or more genes were added from another organism

urea waste product of animals

vector organism that carries and transmits a virus or other agent of disease

Find Out More

Books

Fridell, Ron. *Genetic Engineering: Cool Science.* Minneapolis, MN: Lerner Publications, 2006.

Jones, Phill. *Stem Cell Research and Other Cell-related Controversies.* New York, NY: Chelsea House Publications, 2011.

Kafka, Tina. *Genetic Engineering: Hot Topics.* San Diego, CA: Lucent, 2009.

Keyser, Amber. *Decoding Genes with Max Axiom.* Mankato, MN: Capstone Press, 2010.

Maskell, Hazel and Larkum, Adam. *What's Biology All About?* London: Usborne Publishing, 2009.

Morgan, Sally. *Body Doubles: Cloning Plants and Animals.* Chicago, IL: Heinemann Library, 2009.

Solway, Andrew. *Using Genetic Technology.* Chicago, IL: Heinemann Library, 2008.

Tagliaferro, Linda. *Genetic Engineering: Modern Progress or Future Peril?* Minneapolis, MN: Twenty-first Century Books, 2009.

Winston, Robert. *Evolution Revolution.* New York, NY: DK Publishing, 2009.

Winston, Robert. *What Makes Me, Me?* New York, NY: DK Publishing, 2009.

Websites

www.iptv.org/exploremore/ge
From Iowa Public Television comes this companion website to a television documentary.

www.dnai.org
This website is devoted to DNA: how it was discovered, how it works, and how it affects your life.

www.sciencemuseum.org.uk/WhoAmI/FindOutMore/Yourgenes.aspx
This website shows an animated explanation of how and why your genes make you unique.

http://kidshealth.org/teen
Search this website for articles on genes, genetic disorders, or any other health topic that interests you.

www.eurekascience.com
Click the links on this website to learn about DNA, cloning, and other science topics.

http://learn.genetics.utah.edu/content/tech/cloning
This site provides interactive introductions to cloning. You can even try it yourself in the mouse cloning laboratory.

Index